I0820866

I'm Thinking of a House Pet

Bela Davis

Abdo Kids Junior
is an Imprint of Abdo Kids
abdobooks.com

abdobooks.com

Published by Abdo Kids, a division of ABDO, P.O. Box 398166, Minneapolis, Minnesota 55439.

Printed in the United States of America, North Mankato, Minnesota.

052024

092024

THIS BOOK CONTAINS RECYCLED MATERIALS

Photo Credits: Getty Images, Shutterstock

Production Contributors: Teddy Borth, Jennie Forsberg, Grace Hansen

Design Contributors: Candice Keimig, Pakou Moua

Library of Congress Control Number: 2023948541

Publisher's Cataloging-in-Publication Data

Names: Davis, Bela, author.

Title: I'm thinking of a house pet / by Bela Davis

Description: Minneapolis, Minnesota : Abdo Kids, 2025 | Series: I'm thinking of an animal | Includes online resources and index.

Identifiers: ISBN 9798384900542 (lib. bdg.) | ISBN 9798384901242 (ebook) | ISBN 9798384901594 (Read-to-me eBook)

Subjects: LCSH: Pets--Juvenile literature. | Questions and answers--Juvenile literature. | Riddles--Juvenile literature. | Animals--Juvenile literature. | Zoology--Juvenile literature.

Classification: DDC 636.0887--dc23

Table of Contents

Guess the Animal!

I'm thinking of an animal.

Can you guess what it is?

I'm thinking of an animal that is kept as a pet.

But it is not a dog!

I’m thinking of an animal that is kept inside.

clues

- a pet
- kept inside

But it is not a cat!

I'm thinking of an animal that lays eggs.

clues

- a pet
- kept inside
- lays eggs

But it is not a bird!

I'm thinking of an animal that is kept in a **tank**.

clues

- a pet
- kept inside
- lays eggs
- lives in a tank

But it is not a frog!

I'm thinking of an animal that has no legs.

clues

- a pet
- kept inside
- lays eggs
- lives in a tank
- has scales
- has no legs

But it is not a fish!

Do you know what animal

I'm thinking of?

clues

- a pet
- kept inside
- lays eggs
- lives in a tank
- has scales
- has no legs

I'm thinking of a snake! Now it's your turn! What animal are you thinking of?

Comparing Animals

	bird	frog	turtle	snake
lays eggs	✓	✓	✓	✓
kept in a tank		✓	✓	✓
scales			✓	✓
no legs				✓

Glossary

scale
one of the many small, hard, thin plates that cover fish, reptiles, and certain other animals.

tank
a closed container for keeping small animals. A tank is usually made of clear glass or plastic.

Index